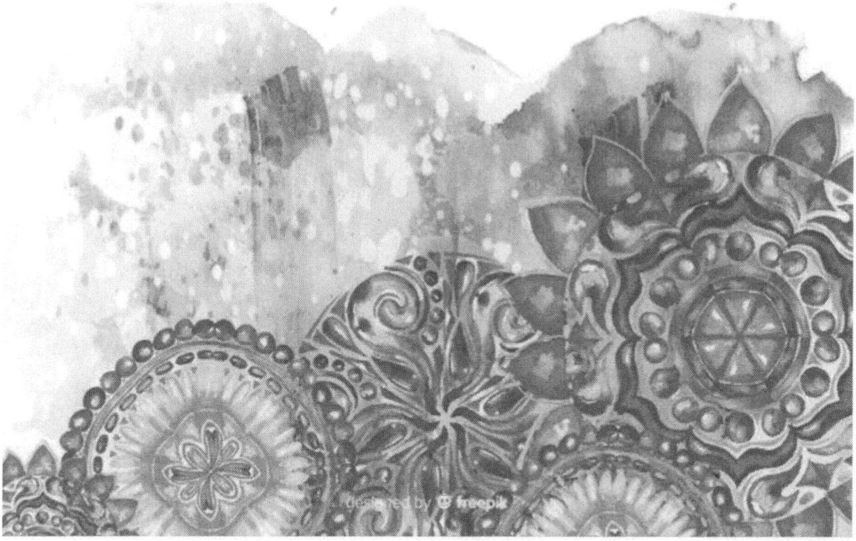

First Name:

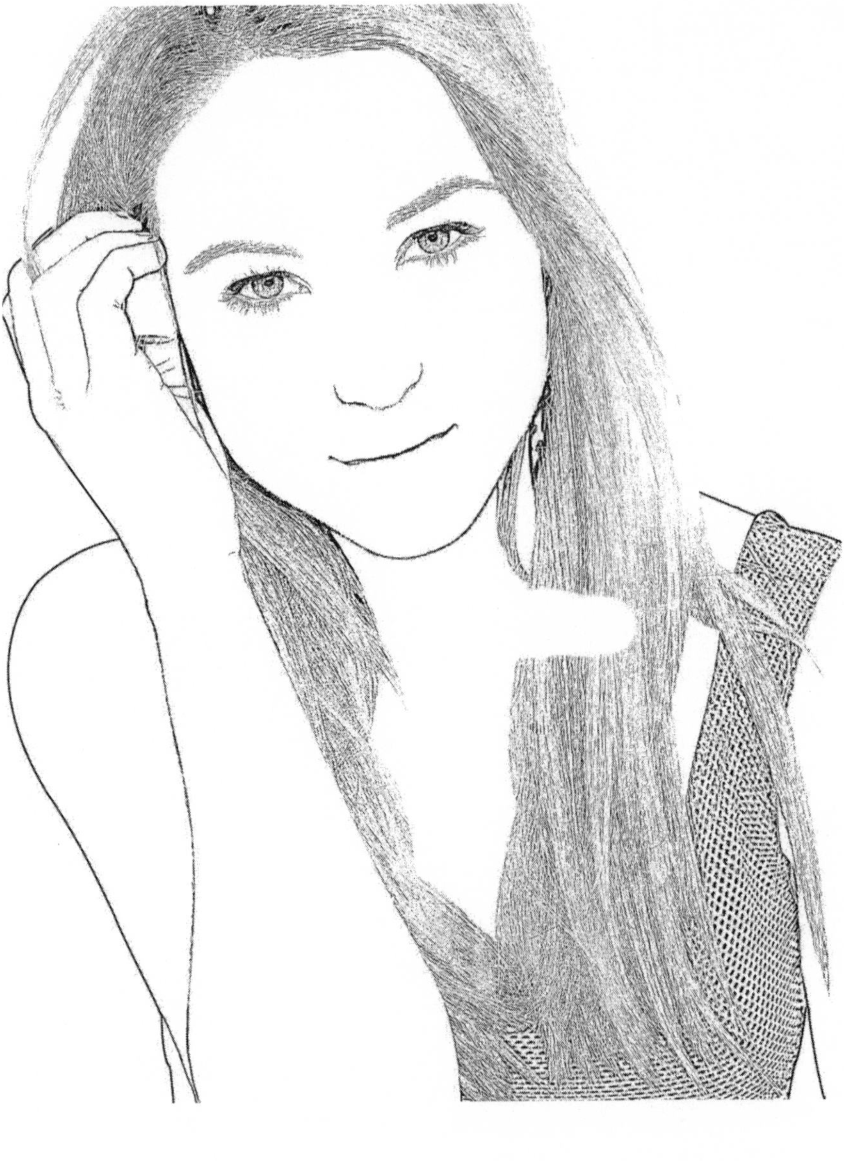

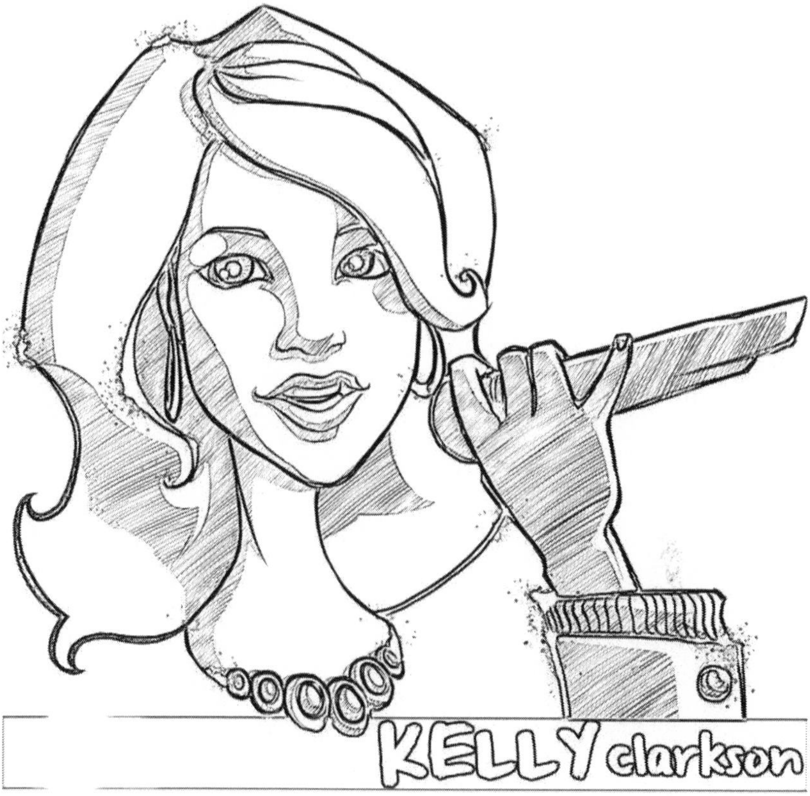
KELLY clarkson

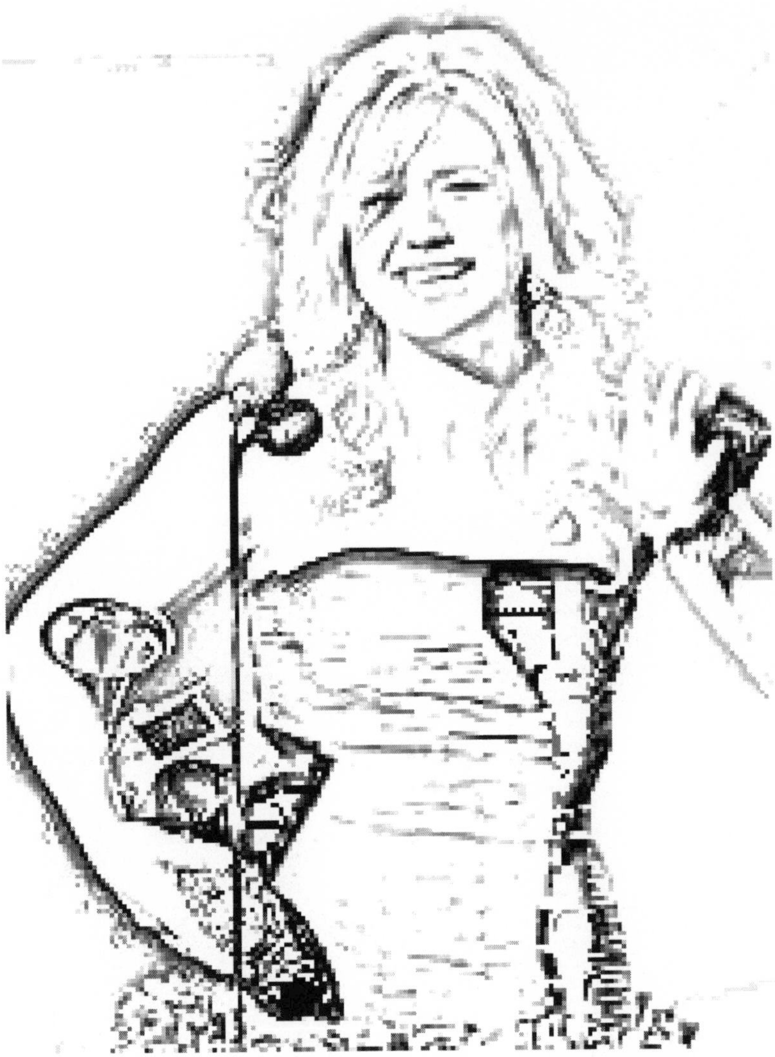

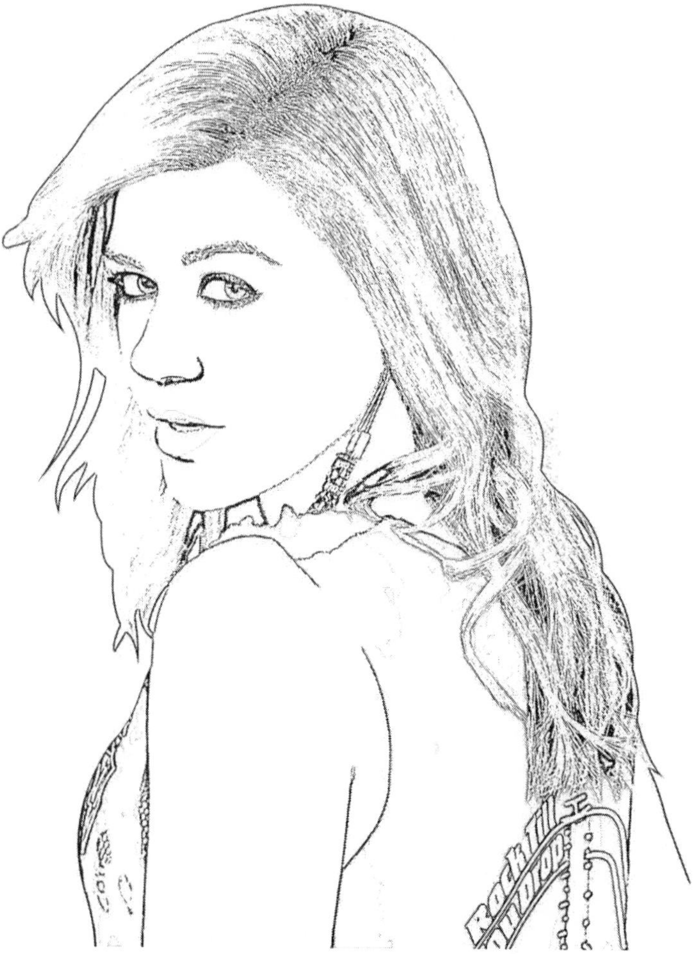
Rock Till

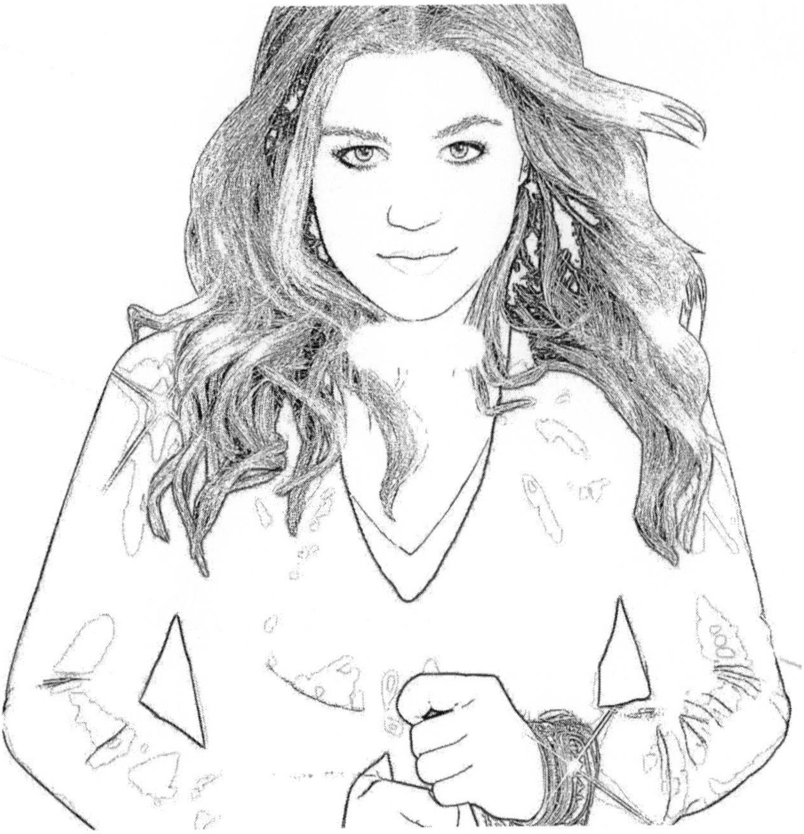

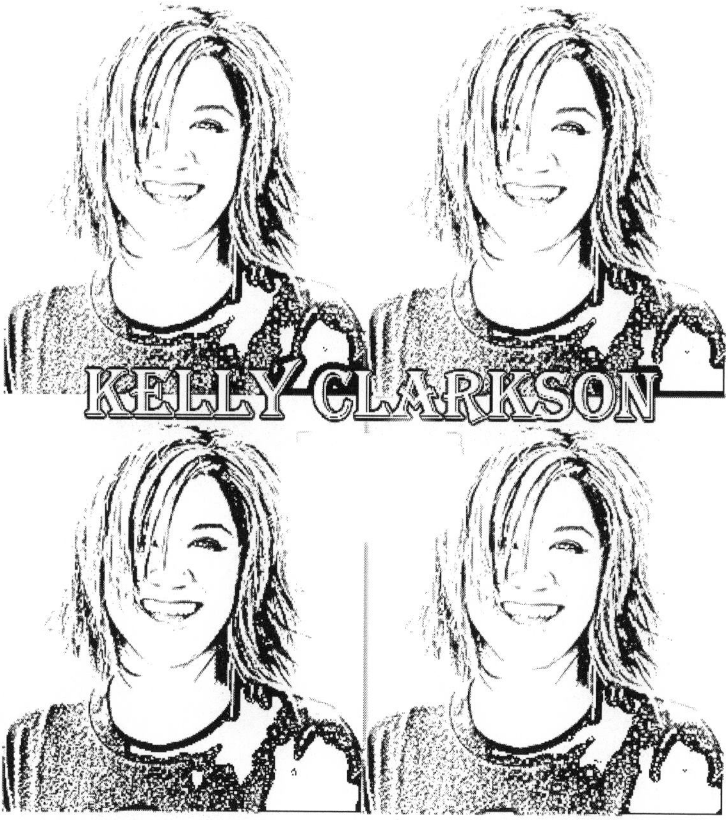
KELLY CLARKSON

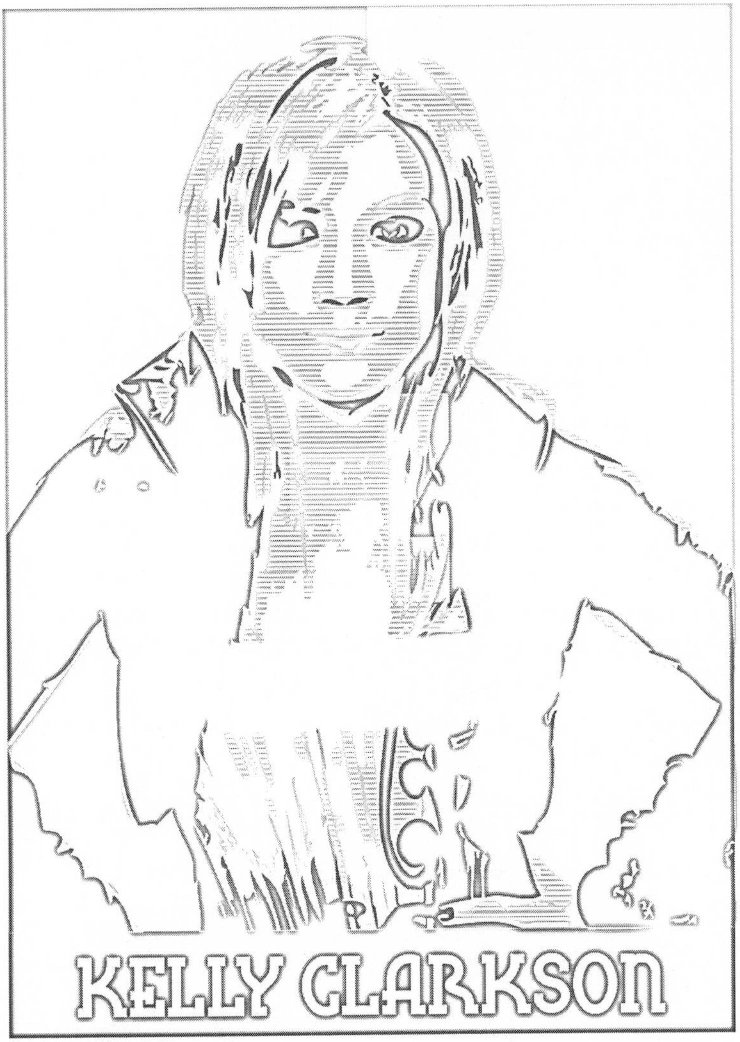
KELLY CLARKSON

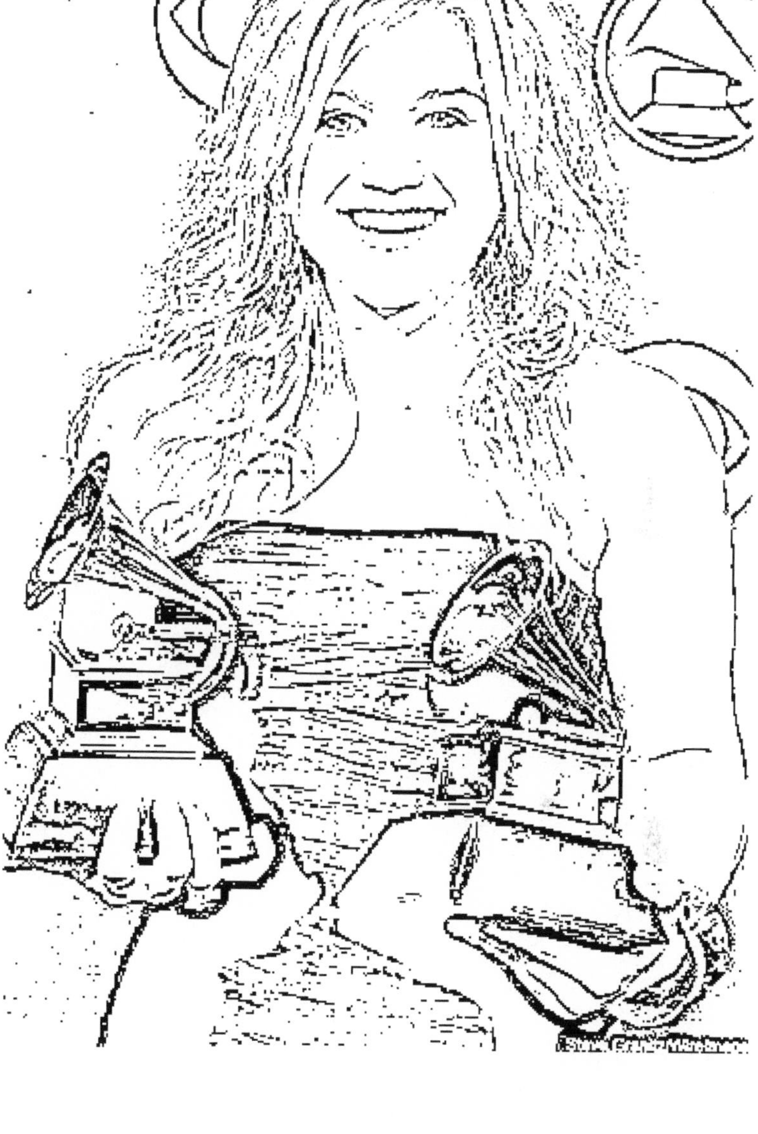

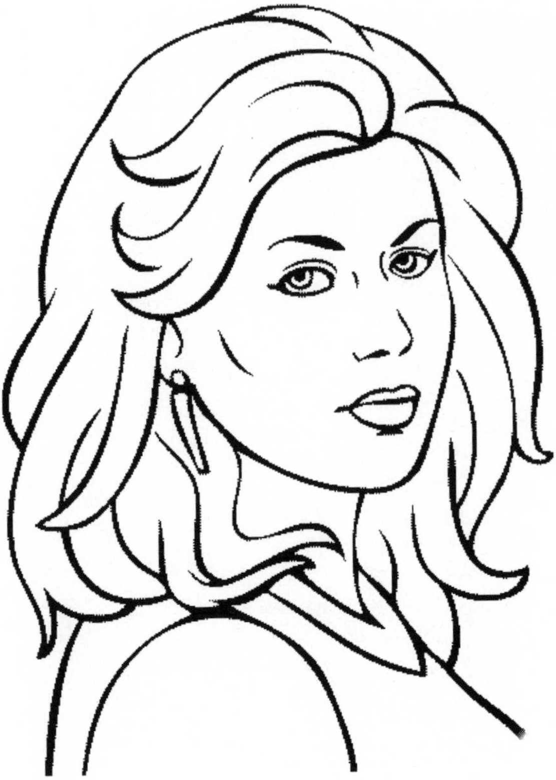

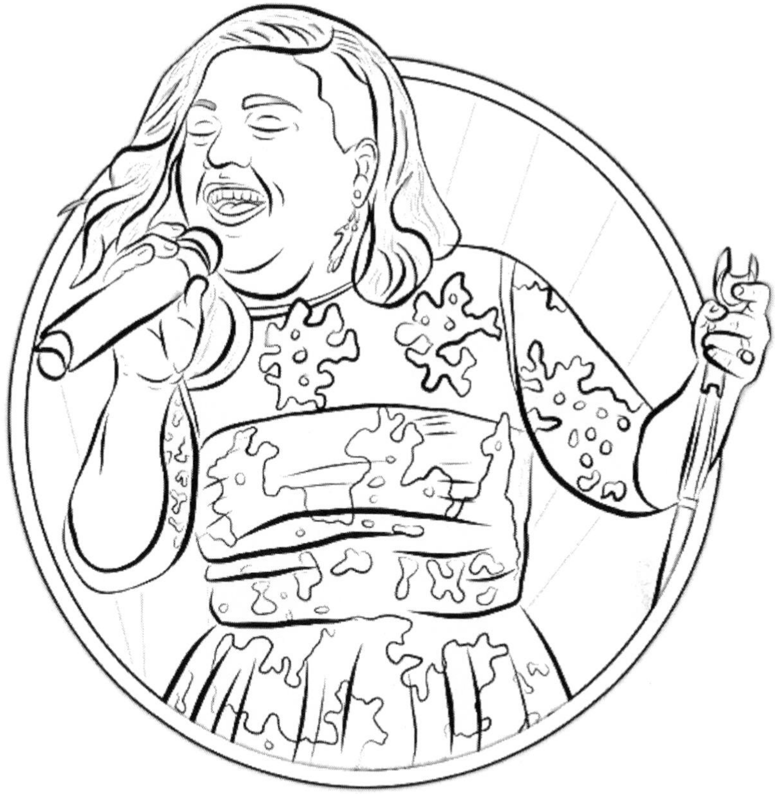

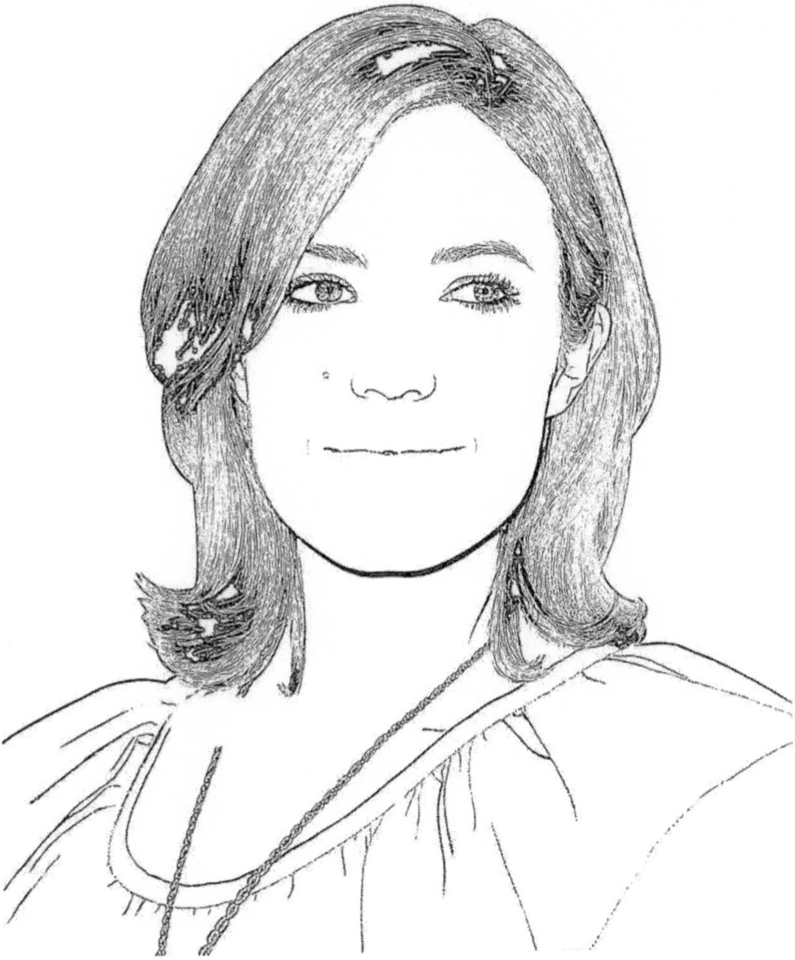

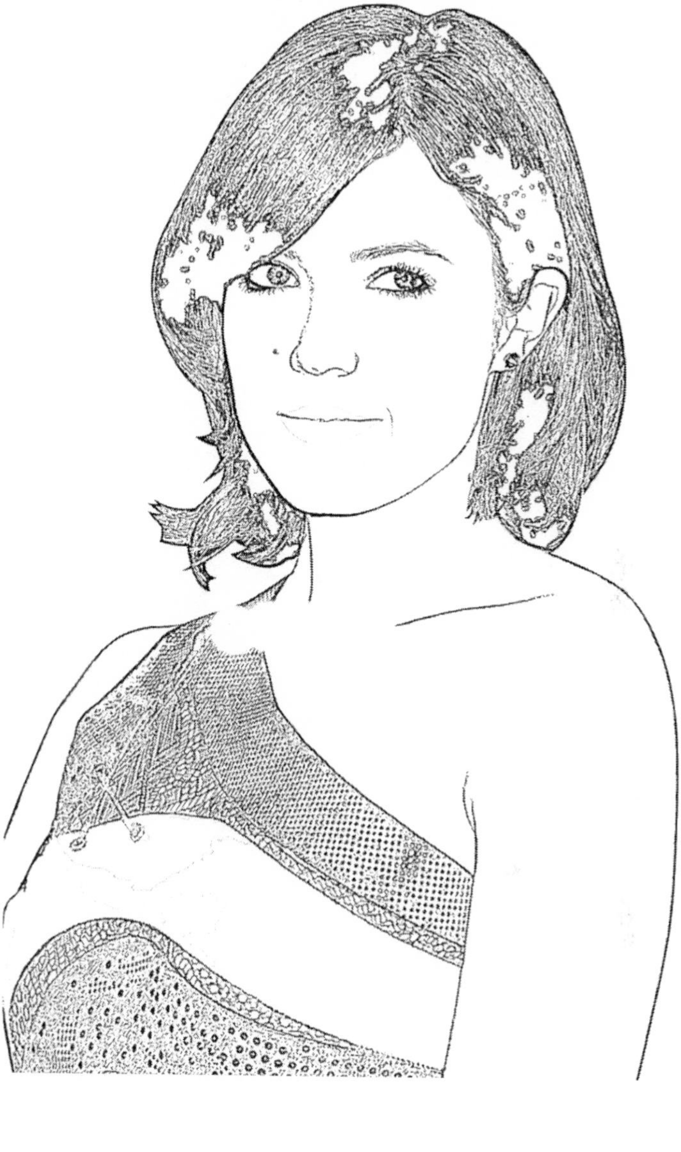

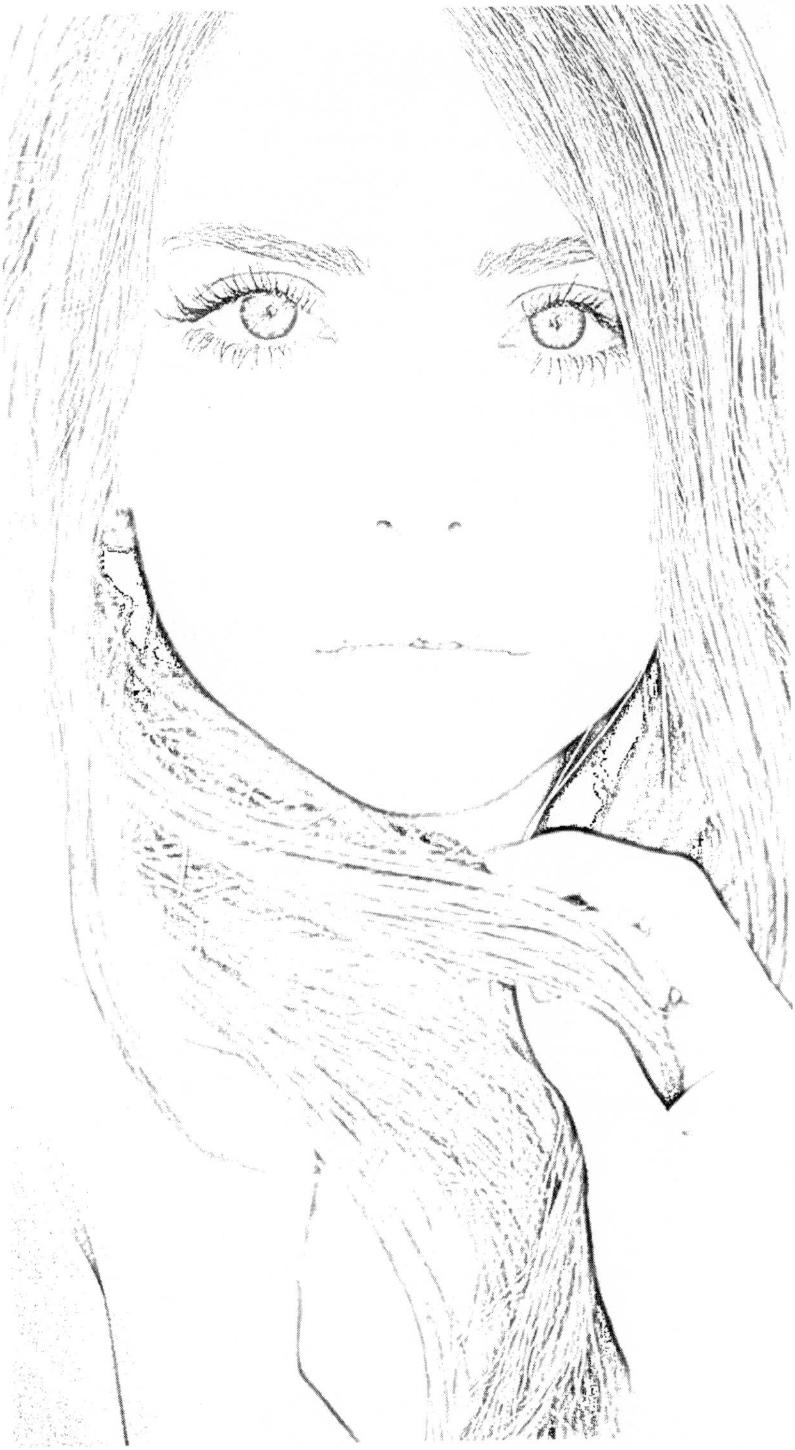

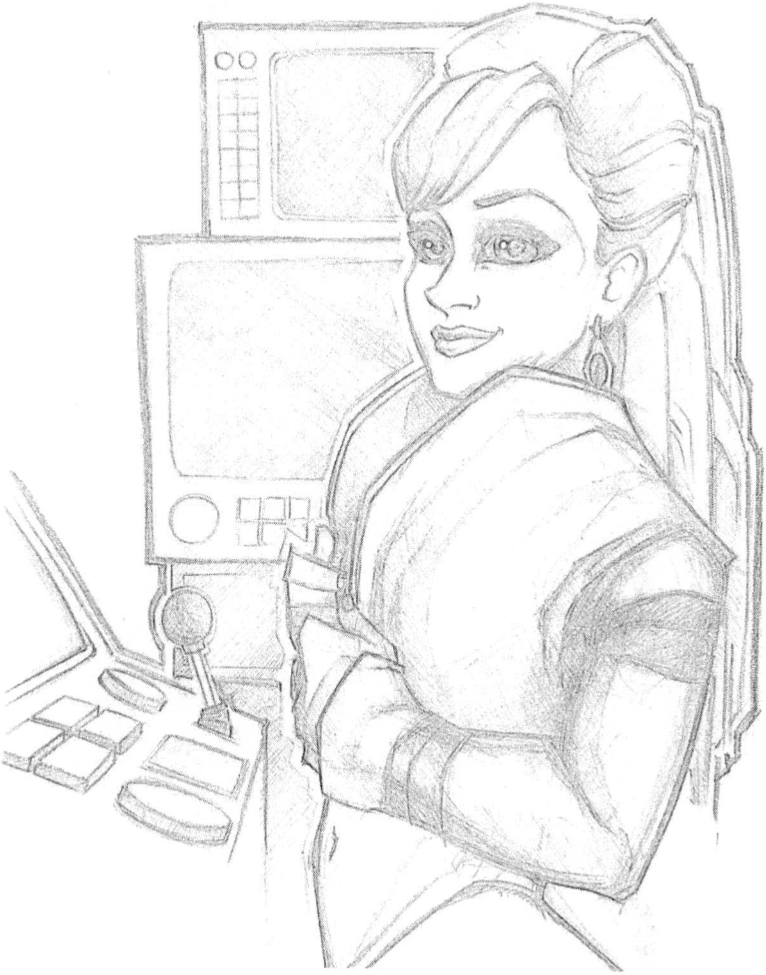

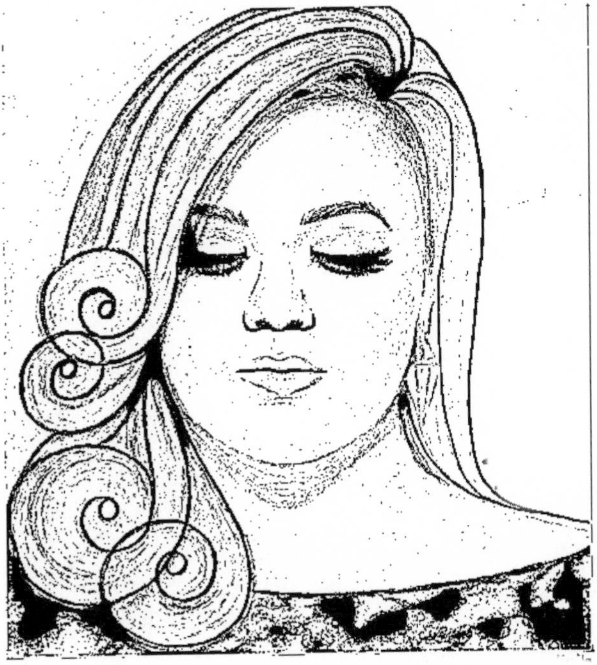

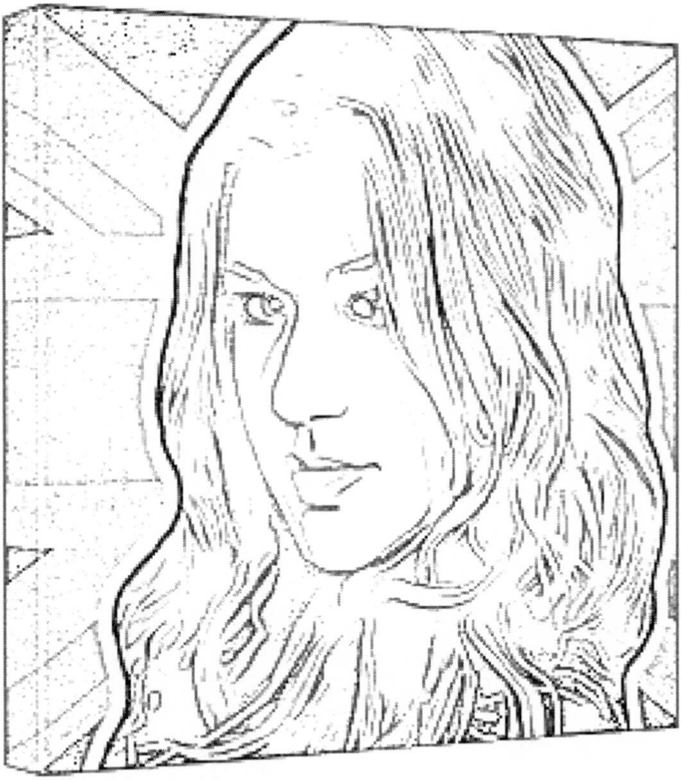

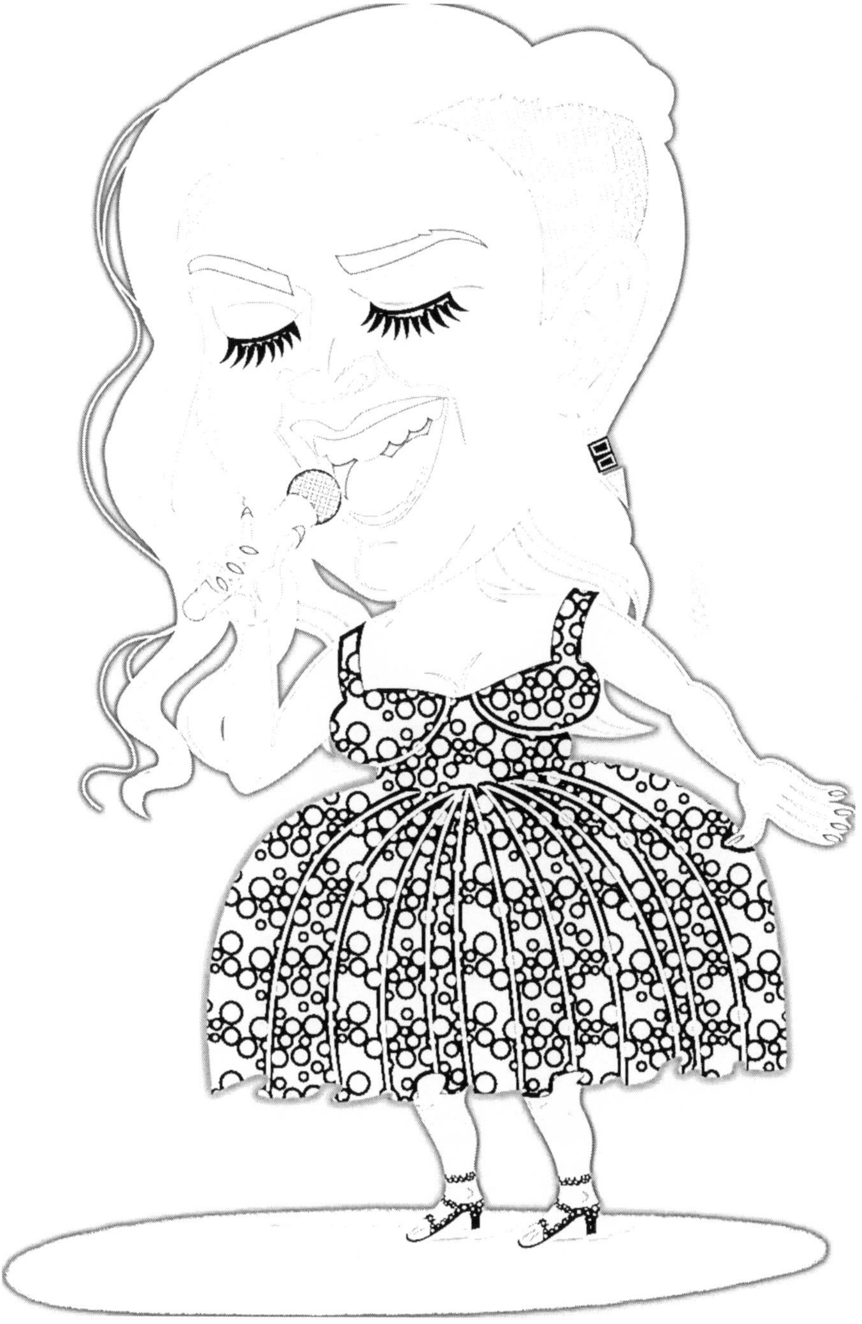

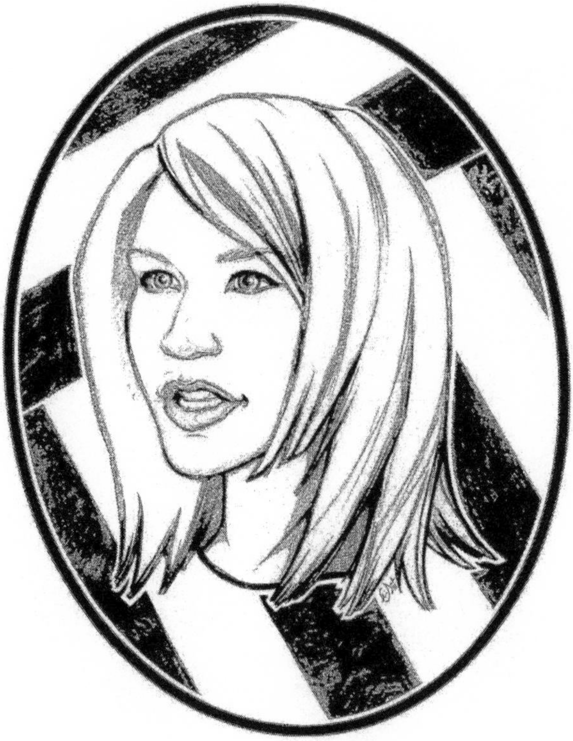

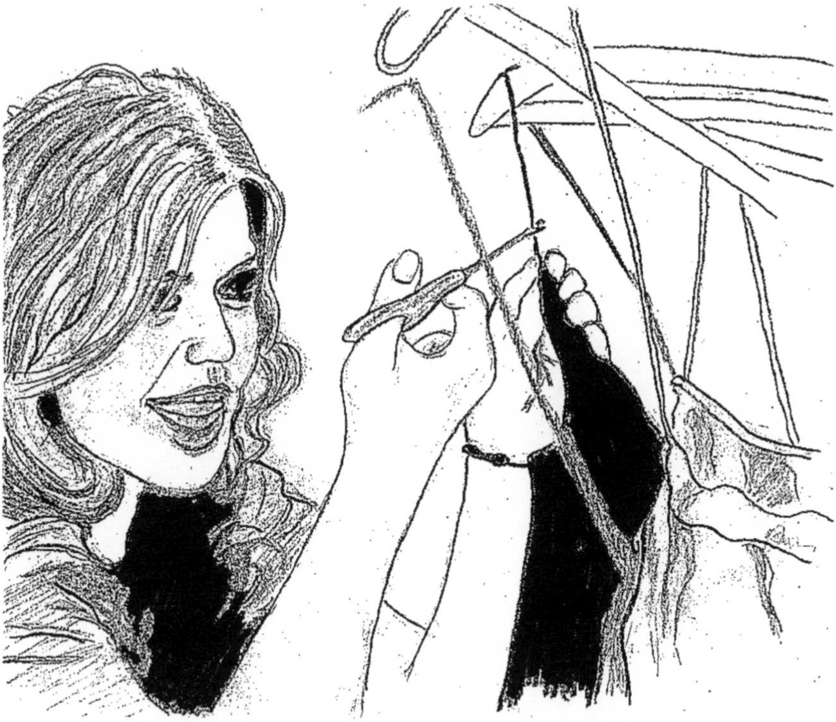

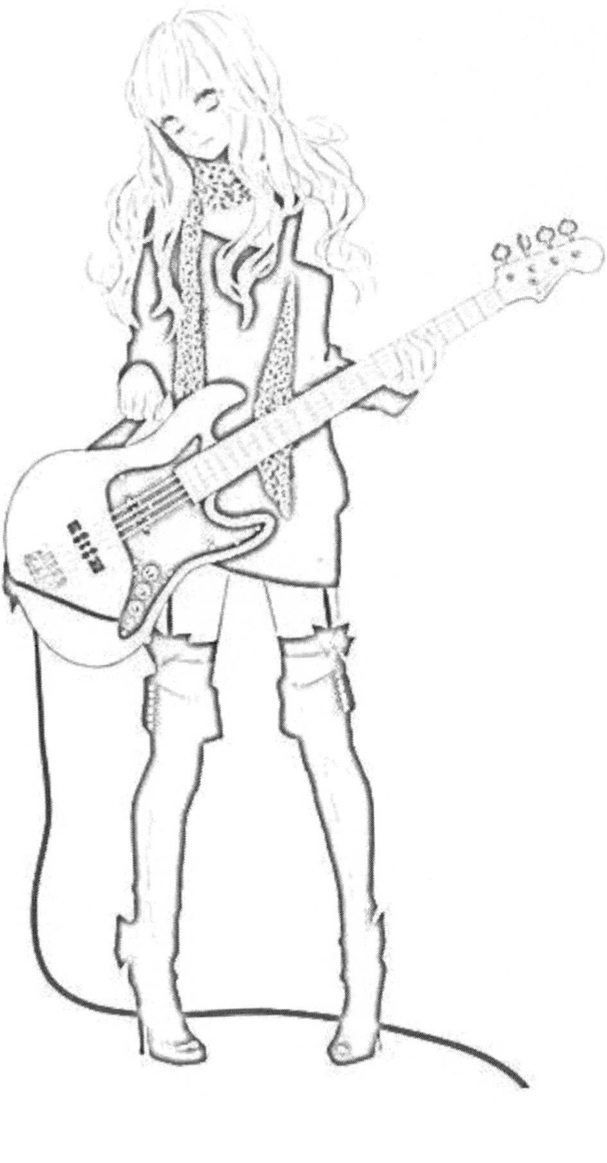

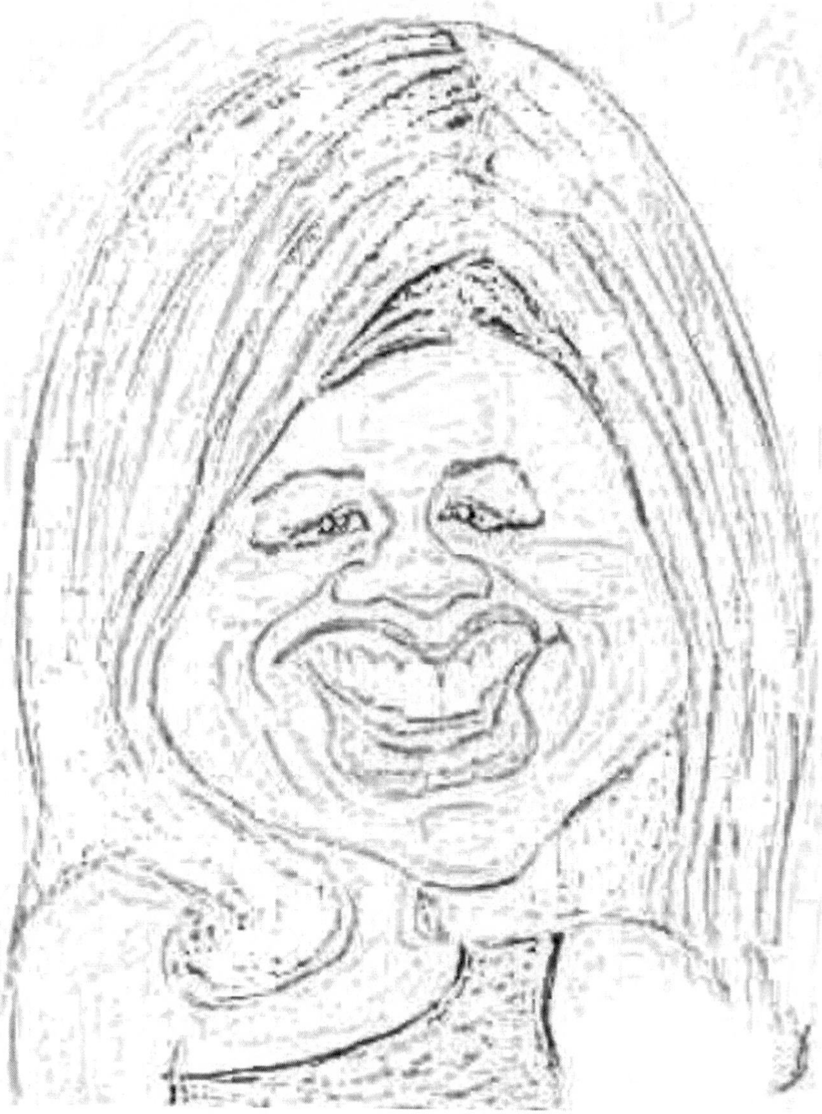

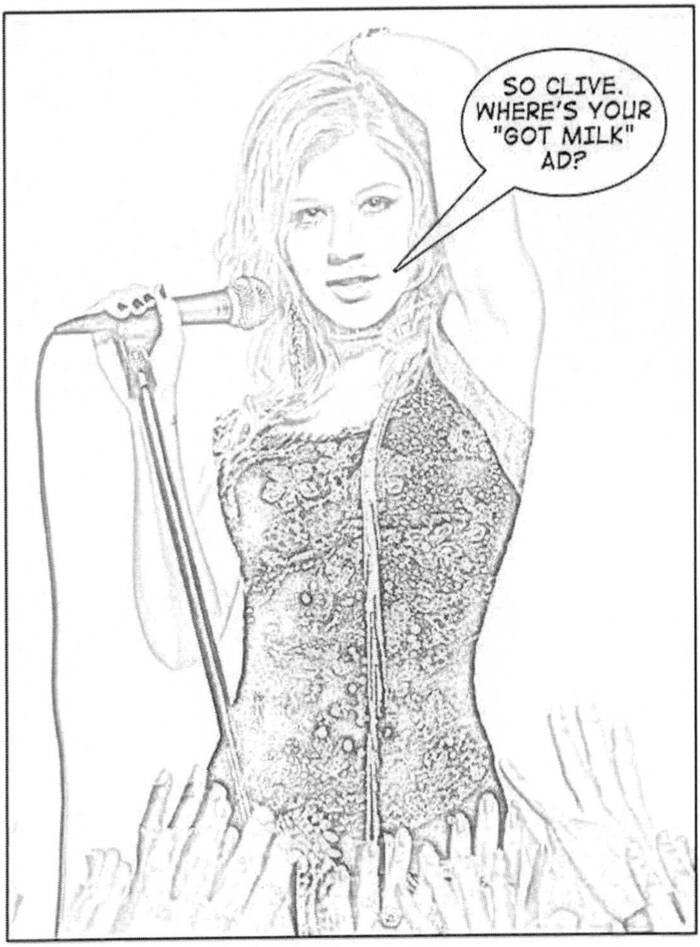
SO CLIVE. WHERE'S YOUR "GOT MILK" AD?

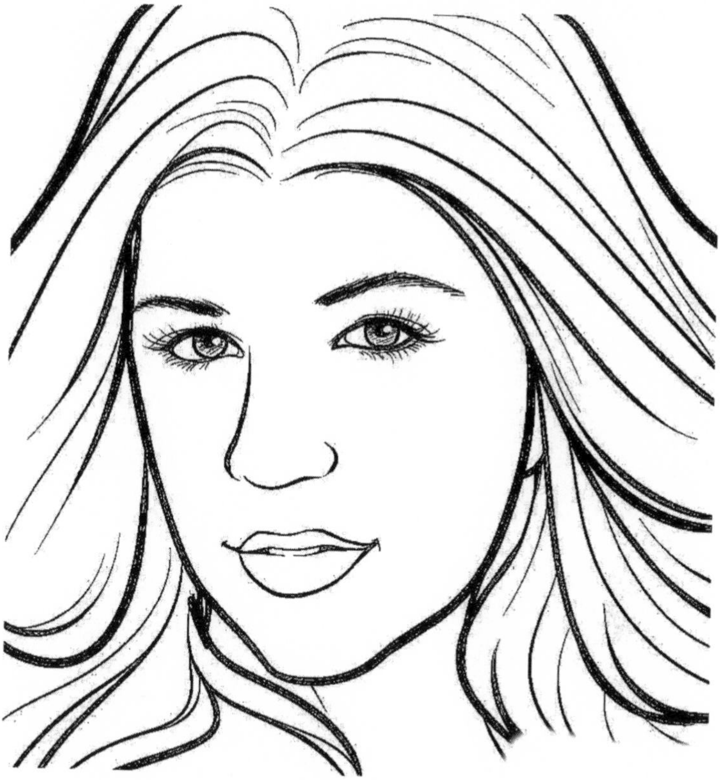

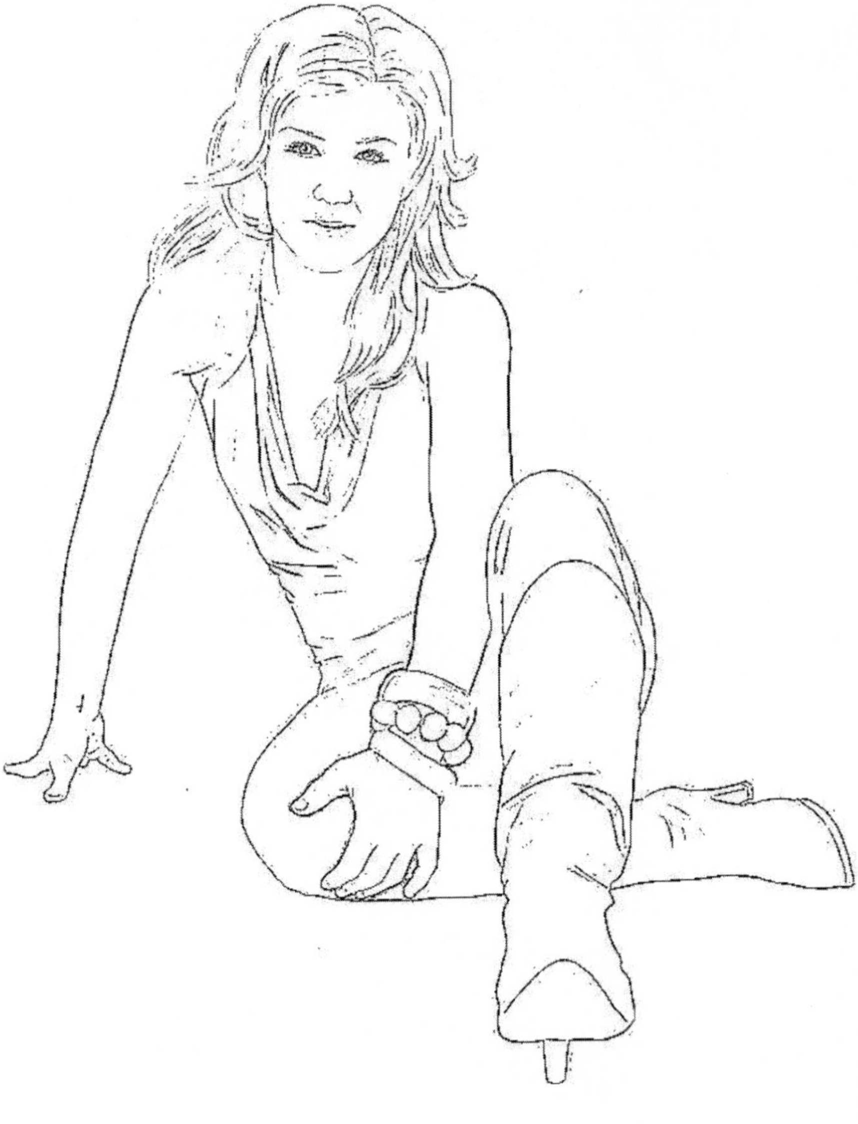

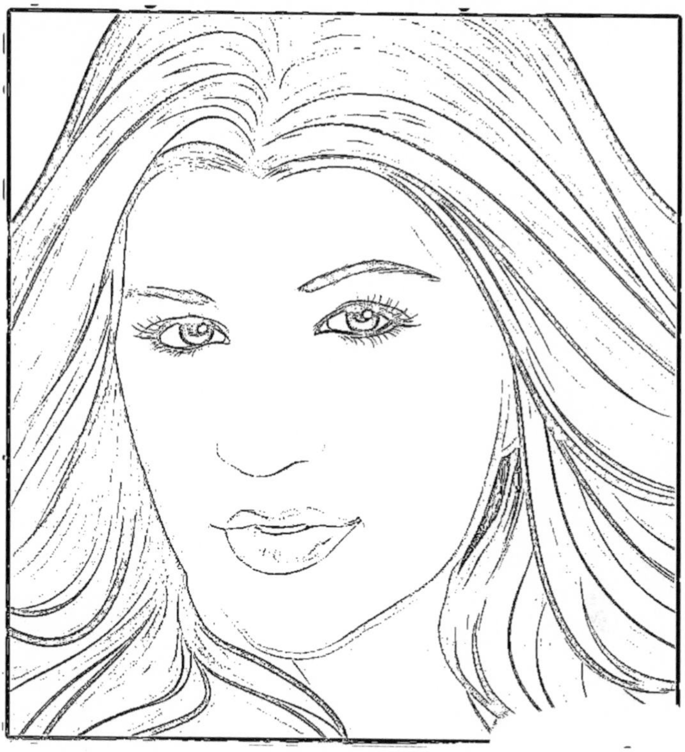

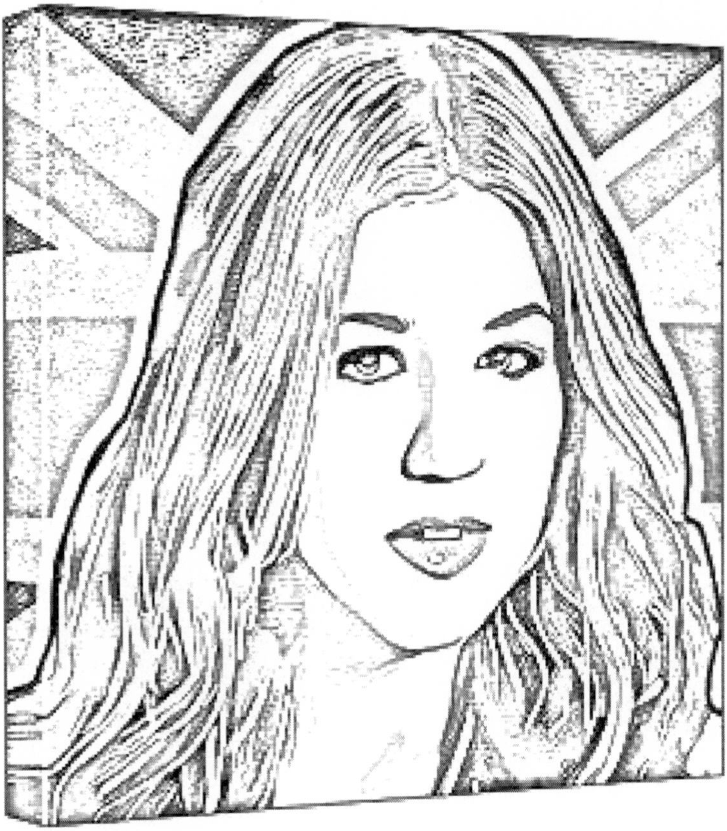

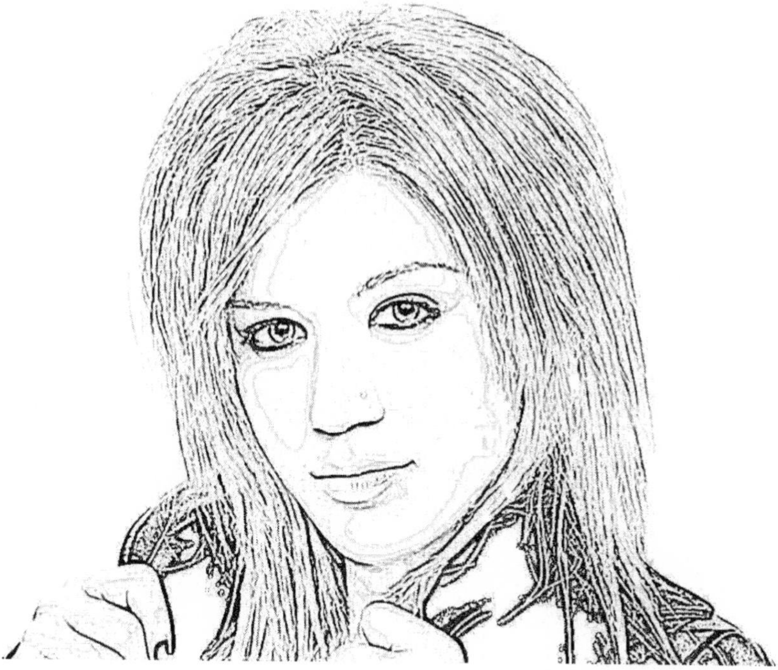

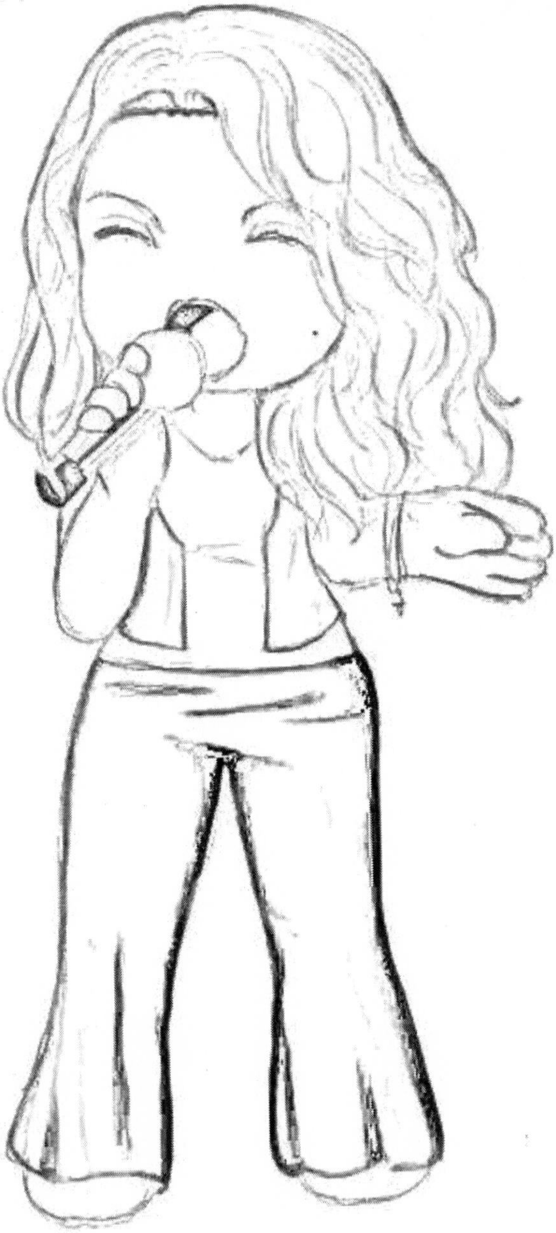

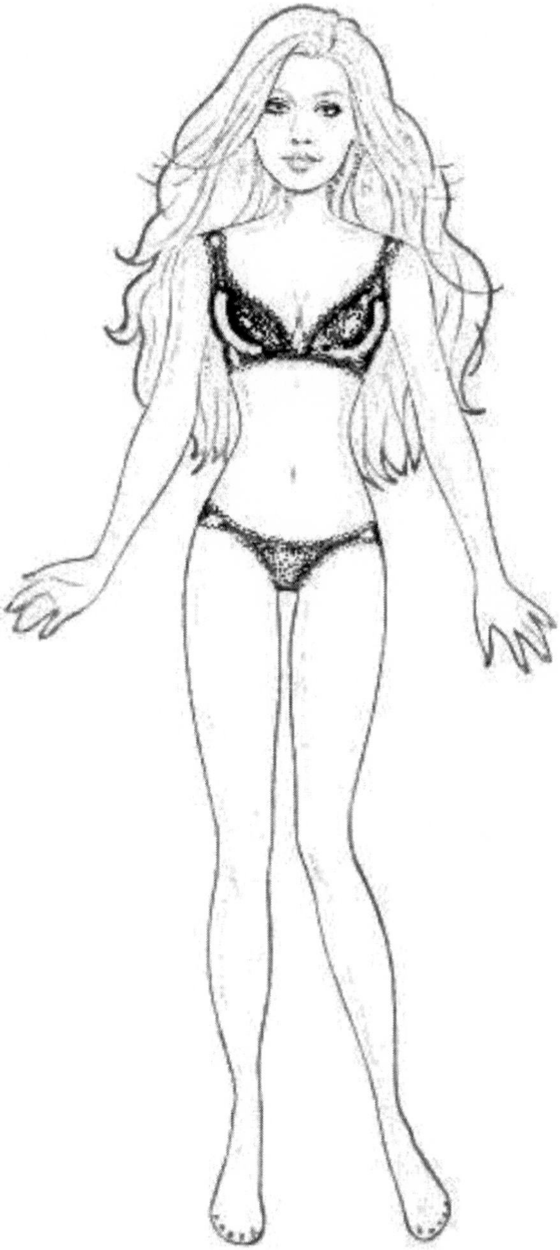

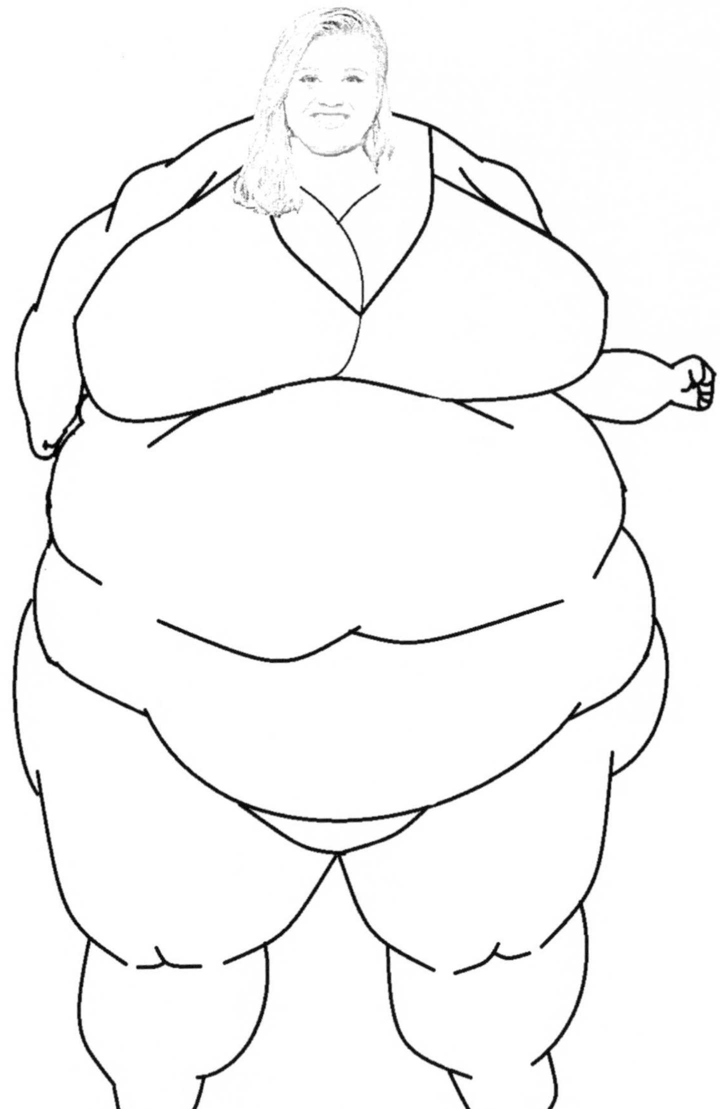

Made in the USA
Monee, IL
08 November 2022

17335535R00021